Cats

Maine Coon Cats

Leo Statts

Launch!
An Imprint of Abdo Zoom
abdobooks.com

abdobooks.com

Published by Abdo Zoom, a division of ABDO, PO Box 398166, Minneapolis, Minnesota 55439.

Printed in the United States of America, North Mankato, Minnesota.

052019
092019

THIS BOOK CONTAINS RECYCLED MATERIALS

Photo Credits: iStock, Shutterstock

Production Contributors: Kenny Abdo, Jennie Forsberg, Grace Hansen, John Hansen

Design Contributors: Dorothy Toth, Neil Klinepier

Library of Congress Control Number: 2018963138

Publisher's Cataloging-in-Publication Data

Names: Statts, Leo, author.

Title: Maine coon cats / by Leo Statts.

Description: Minneapolis, Minnesota : Abdo Zoom, 2020 | Series: Cats | Includes online resources and index.

Identifiers: ISBN 9781532127106 (lib. bdg.) | ISBN 9781532128080 (ebook) | ISBN 9781532128578 (Read-to-me ebook)

Subjects: LCSH: Maine coon cat--Juvenile literature. | Cat, Domestic--Juvenile literature. | Cats--Behavior--Juvenile literature. | Cat breeds--Juvenile literature.

Classification: DDC 636.8--dc23

Table of Contents

Maine Coon Cats

Maine coon cats make great family pets. They are kind and **gentle**.

Maine coons are larger than most cat **breeds**.

Body

Maine coons have thick and pretty fur.

The fur keeps them warm in cold weather.

Maine coons can be many different colors.

They do not meow. They make a **chirping** noise instead.

Maine coons are fully grown within four to five years. They live for about 12 years.

Care

A Maine coon's fur should be brushed once a week. This keeps it from becoming messy and tangled.

Maine coons also need scratching posts. They have a natural urge to scratch.

Maine coons need a litter box. It should be kept clean.

Personality

Maine coons are **energetic** and friendly. They get along with everyone, even dogs!

Maine coons like water. They are good swimmers.

History

Maine coons were first bred in New England. They are the official cat **breed** of Maine.

Maine coons have been around since the 1800s.

Quick Stats

Average Weight

A Maine coon cat is lighter than a bowling ball.

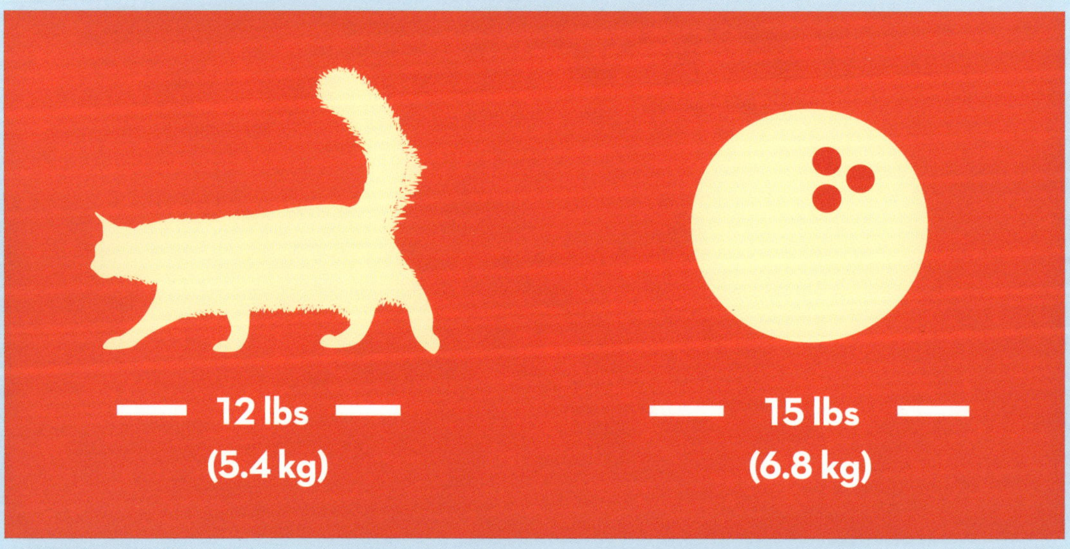

Quick Stats

Average Height

A Maine coon cat is slightly taller than a basketball.

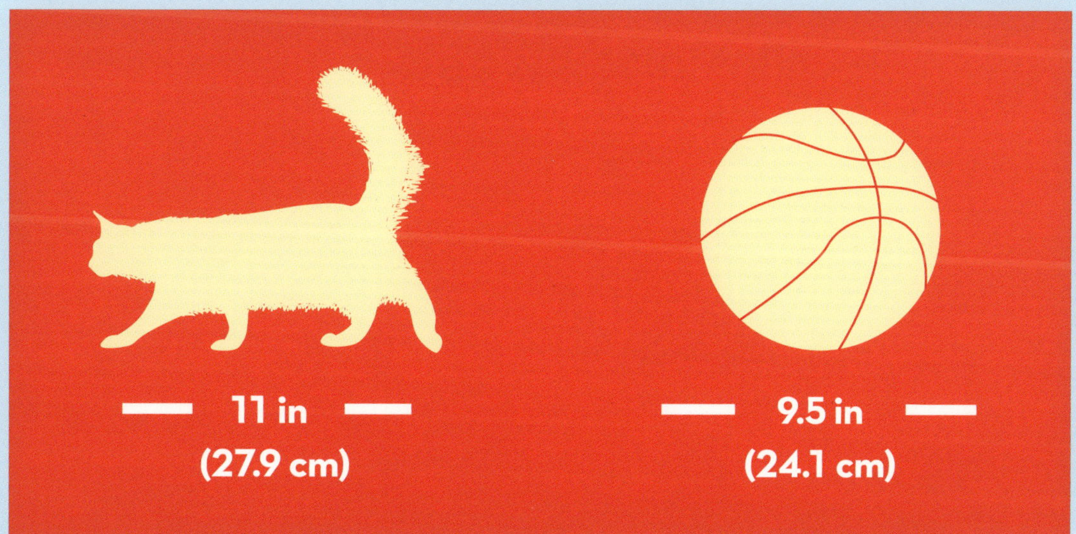

Glossary

breed – a group of animals sharing the same looks and features.

chirp – a short, sharp, high-pitched sound.

energetic – active and full of energy.

gentle – calm and sweet.

Online Resources

Booklinks
NONFICTION NETWORK
FREE! ONLINE NONFICTION RESOURCES

For more information on Maine coon cats here, please visit **abdobooklinks.com** or scan this QR code.

Abdo Zoom
DATABASES
BEGINNING ONLINE RESEARCH

Learn even more with the Abdo Zoom Animals database. Visit **abdozoom.com** today!

Index